•Bartholo[mew]

SWINDON
Streetfinder
COLOUR ATLAS

CONTENTS

Bartholomew
An Imprint of HarperCollins*Publishers*

Bartholomew Swindon Streetfinder Colour Atlas

Bartholomew
An Imprint of Harper Collins*Publishers*
77-85 Fulham Palace Road, Hammersmith, London W6 8JB

Printed in Hong Kong
ISBN 0 7028 3271 5
JI 8481   ANE

KEY TO MAP SYMBOLS

M4 Motorway	—— Postal District Boundary	Leisure & Tourism
Dual A419 Primary Route	Bus/Coach Station	Shopping
Dual A361 'A' Road	P Car Park	Administration & Law
Dual B4006 'B' Road	i Tourist Information Centre	Health & Welfare
Other Road	WC Public Toilet	Education
Pedestrian Street	Pol Police Station	Industry & Commerce
Cycle Path	PO Post Office	Park/Garden/ Sports Ground
Track	Lib Library	Public Open Space/Allotments
Footpath	Fire Sta Fire Station	Wood/Forest
One Way Street	+ Church	Golf Course
Main British Rail Station	✡ Synagogue	Cemetery
Other British Rail Station	☾ Mosque	

MAIN MAP PAGES

Scale 1:15,000 (4 ¼ inches to 1 mile approx.)

0   0.25   0.50   0.75   1km

0   ¼   ½ mile

A Grid Reference

20 Page Continuation Number

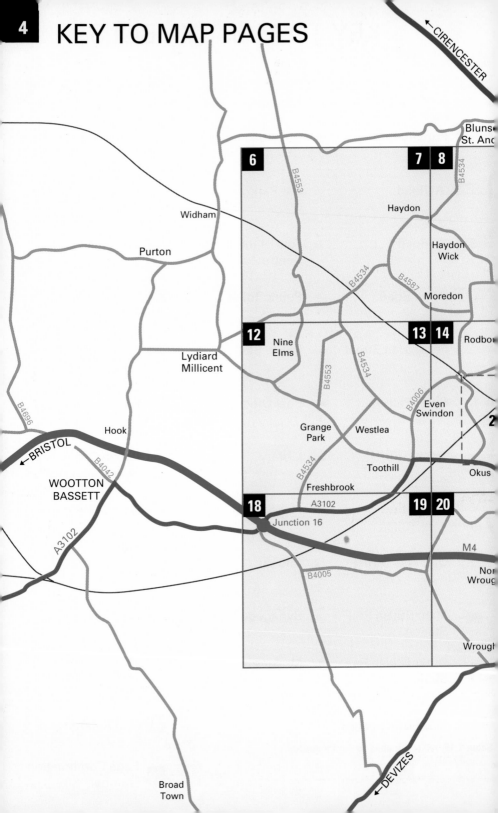

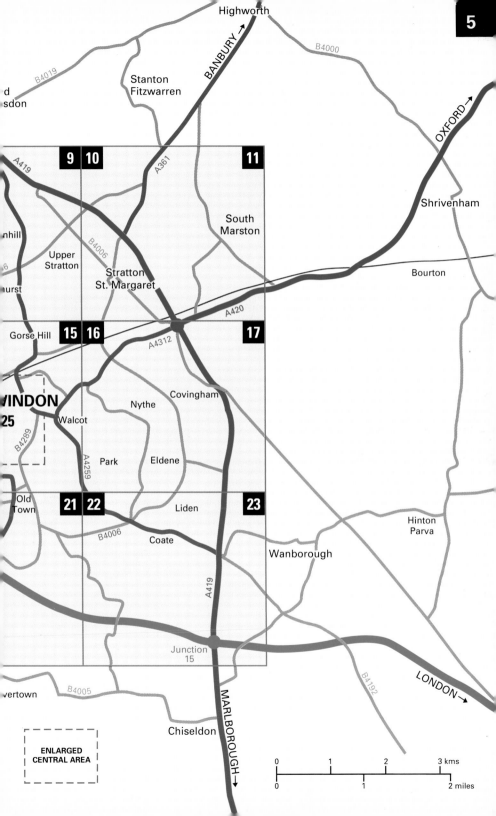

6

A   B   C   D

TADPOLE LANE

1

2

COLLINS   LANE

3

4

THE   HYDE

Bremhill
Bridge

B4553

THE   FOX   B4553

5

Ridgeway Farm

PURTON   ROAD   B4534

SPARCEL
GARLOCK CLO
BUIE
EVIS CLI
ASHE CLO
MELFORT CLO

THE CRESCENT

SWINLEY DRIVE
ETTER ROD
BGE
STOCK CLO
SOU COP
TOWER ROD
CLO
MIDW CLO

6

STONE   LANE

SHOE CRESCENT
EATON END
CRESCENT
CLAY COP
CHASE
WD
FURZE CLO
SPARCELLS
ORRIN CLO
CADLE CLO

A   B   C   D

▼ **12**

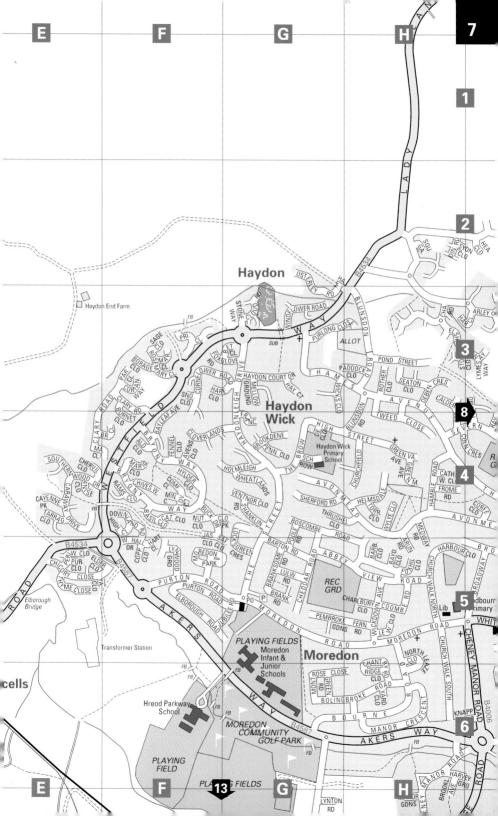

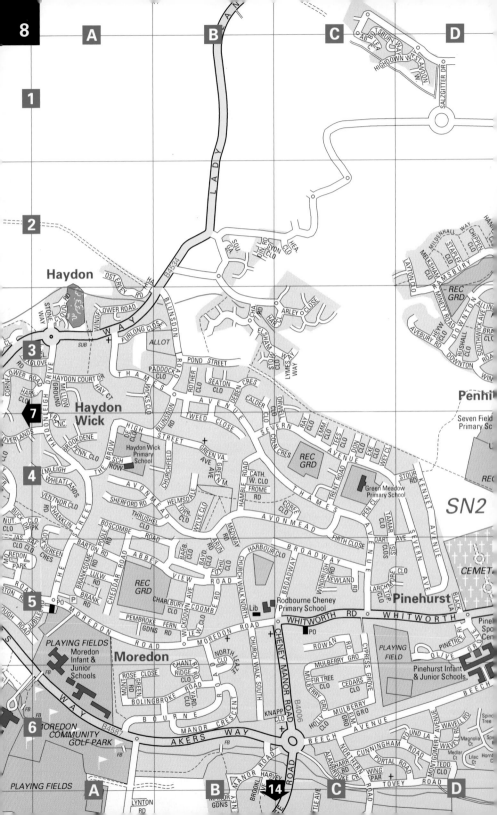

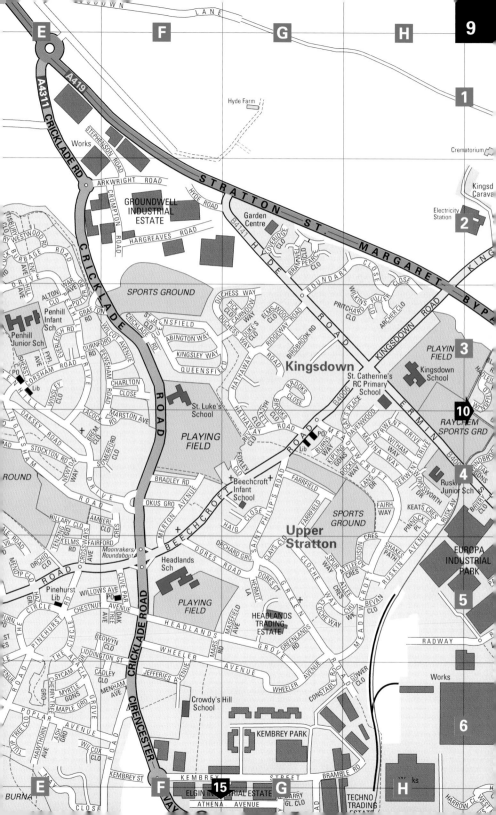

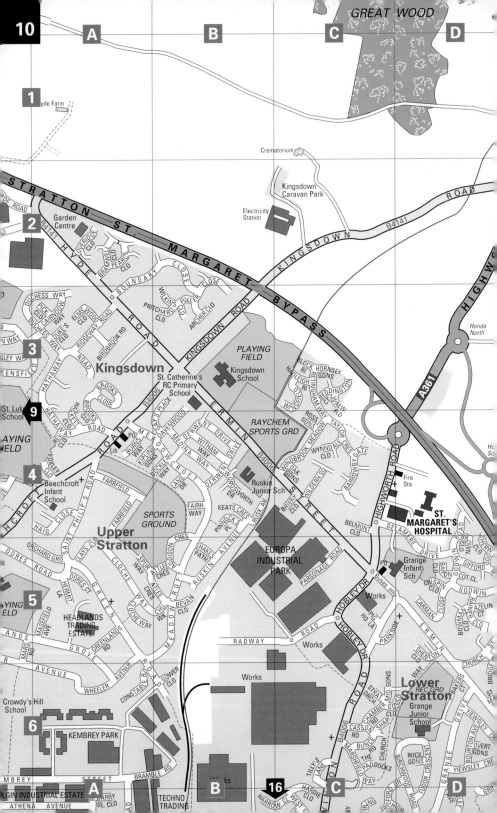

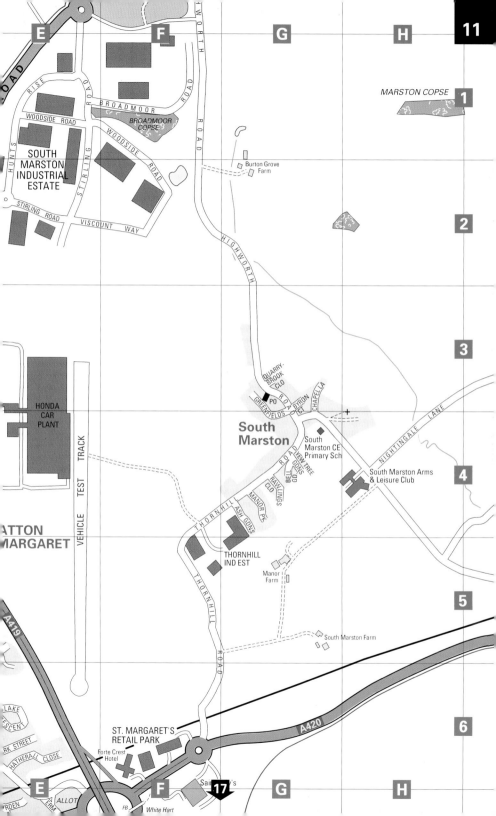

E   F   G   H   **11**

MARSTON COPSE **1**

ROAD

RISE

BROADMOOR
ROAD

WOODSIDE ROAD

BROADMOOR
COPSE

WOODSIDE ROAD

STIRLING ROAD

HUNTS

SOUTH
MARSTON
INDUSTRIAL
ESTATE

STIRLING ROAD

VISCOUNT WAY

Burton Grove
Farm

2

HIGHWORTH

3

QUARRY-
BROOK
CLO

PO

GREENFIELDS

ROAD

BYRON
CT

CHAPEL LA

NIGHTINGALE LANE

**South
Marston**

South
Marston CE
Primary Sch

YEW TREE

GDNS

BELL

ROAD

CLO

RAWLINGS

South Marston Arms
& Leisure Club

4

HONDA
CAR
PLANT

VEHICLE TEST TRACK

THORNHILL

ROAD

ASH GDNS

MANOR PK

THORNHILL
IND EST

Manor
Farm

**ATTON
MARGARET**

THORNHILL

ROAD

South Marston Farm

5

A419

A420

6

LAKE
CRESCENT

RK STREET

HATHERALL CLOSE

ST. MARGARET'S
RETAIL PARK

Forte Crest
Hotel

Saint's

17

E   F   G   H

RDEN

ALLOT

FB   White Hart

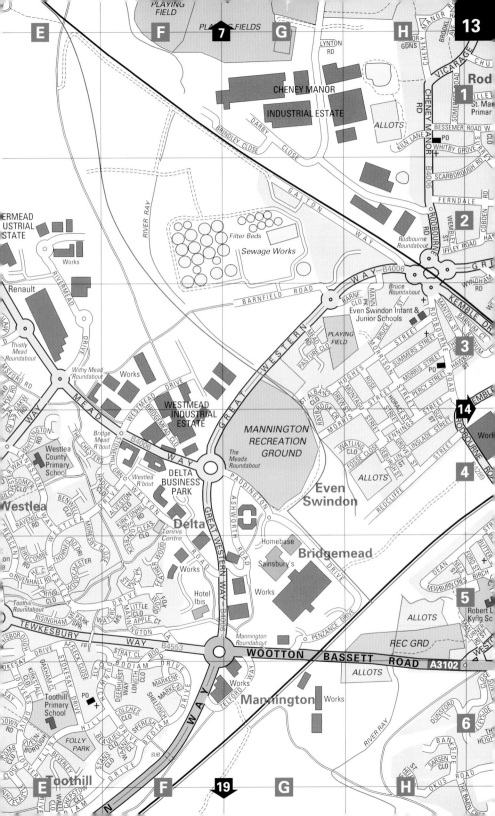

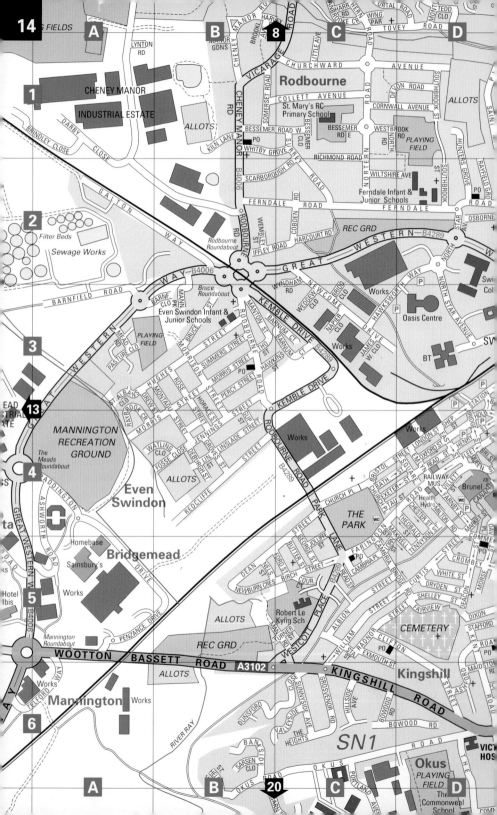

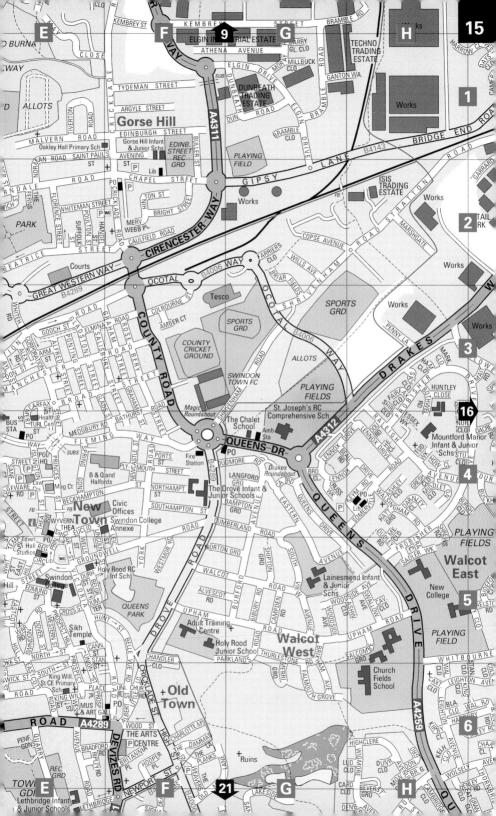

Toothill

WESTERN

South
Leaze

MILL LANE

M4

B4005

WHARF

ROAD

Sewage W

SAVILL CRES
MAUNSELL
WICT CRISS RD
ELLINGDON
KELLSBORO
RD
HOUSE
WAY
B4005
MASKELEYNE
ANTHONY
CLO
RD
PLUM CLO
YSHENCOPSE   RD
BLADEN CLO
WHARF

Elcombe

Wroughton

WHALLE
ELCOMBE   AVE
COWLEAZE CRES
MARK PL

Wrough
Infant S

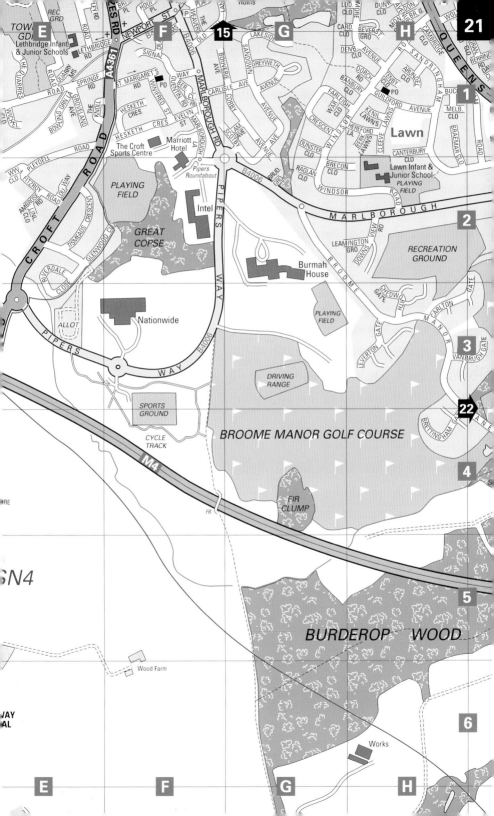

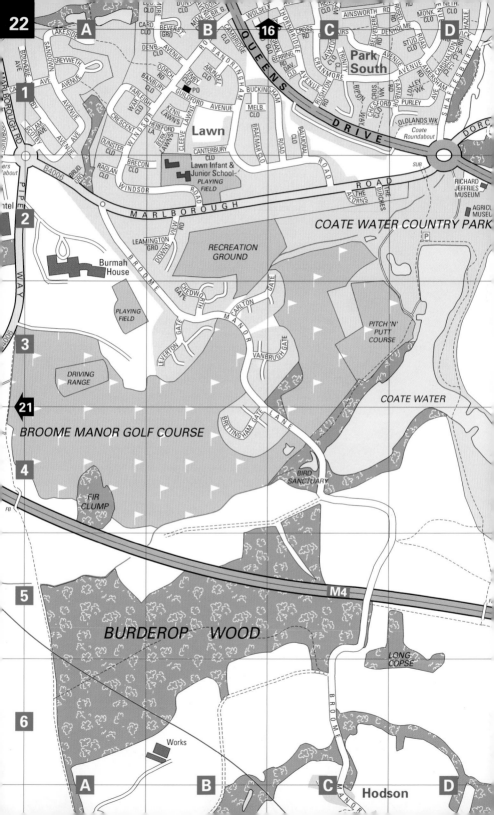

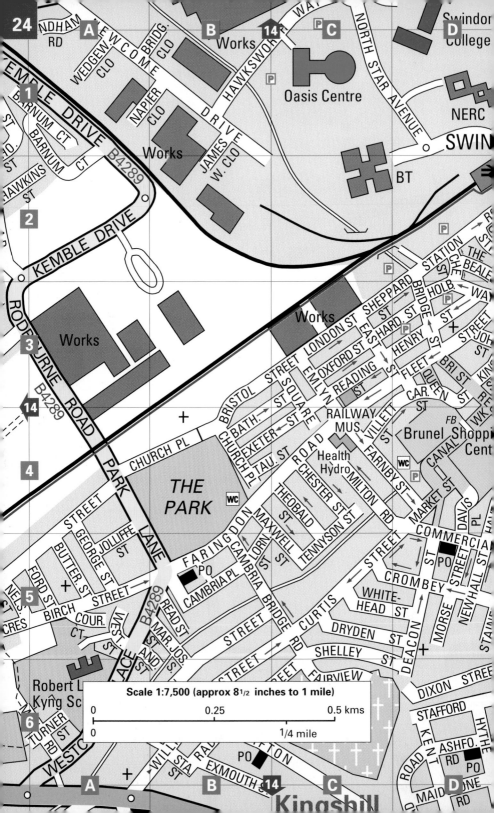

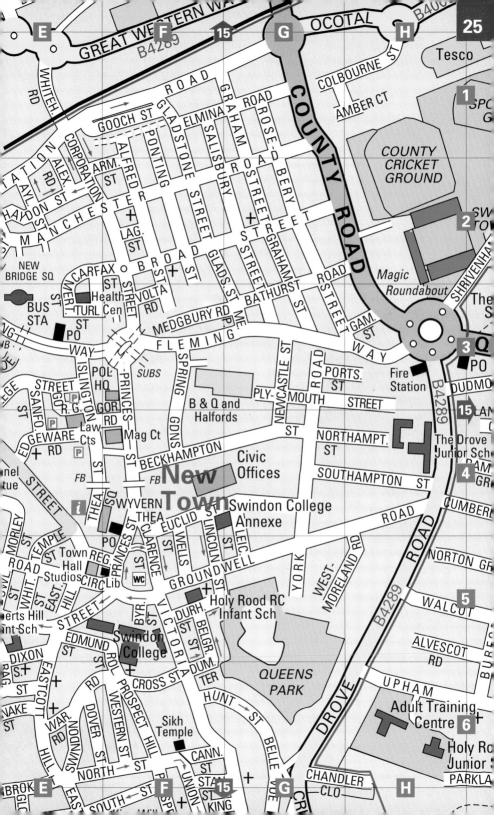

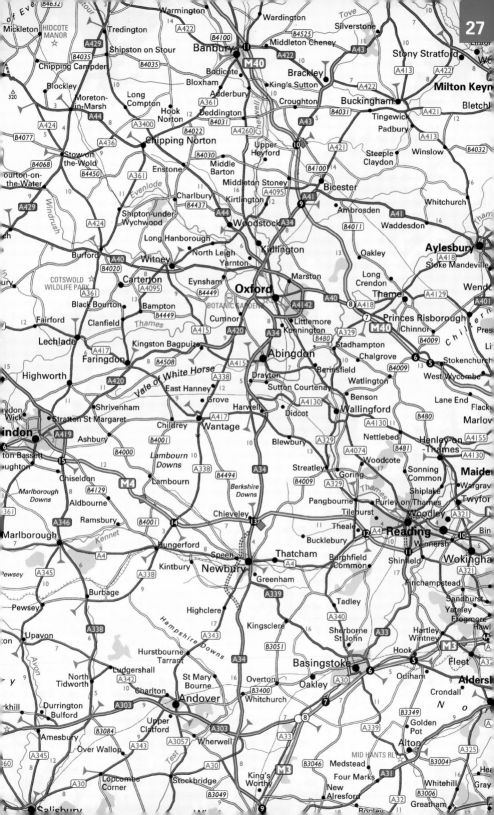

INDEX TO STREETS

General Abbreviations

Av	Avenue	Gdns	Gardens	Pl	Place
Bri	Bridge	Gra	Grange	Rd	Road
Cen	Centre, Central	Grd	Ground	Ri	Rise
Ch	Church	Grn	Green	S	South
Circ	Circle	Gro	Grove	Sch	School
Clo	Close	Ho	House	Sq	Square
Cres	Crescent	Hosp	Hospital	St	Street
Ct	Court	Ind	Industrial	St.	Saint
Dr	Drive	La	Lane	Sta	Station
E	East	Lo	Lodge	Ter	Terrace
Est	Estate	Mkt	Market	Trd	Trading
Fld	Field	Ms	Mews	Vw	View
Flds	Fields	N	North	W	West
Fm	Farm	Par	Parade	Wd	Wood
Gdn	Garden	Pk	Park	Wk	Walk

NOTES

All streets within the Central Swindon enlarged-scale section (pages 24-25) are shown in **bold type** when named in the index, e.g. **Aylesbury St.** will be found on page **25** and in square **E2**.

This index contains some street names in standard text which are followed by another street named in italics. In these cases the street in standard text does not actually appear on the map due to insufficient space but can be located close to the street

Bakers Ct. SN3	10 D6	Benwell Clo. SN5	13 E4	Bosworth Rd. SN5	12 C5
Bale Clo. SN5	12 B5	Berenger Clo. SN3	21 F1	Bothwell Rd. SN3	16 B3
Balmoral Clo. SN3	22 C1	Beresford Clo. SN3	17 E6	Boundary Clo. SN2	9 G3
Bampton Gro. SN3	15 G4	Berkeley Lawns SN3	22 B1	Bourne Rd. SN2	7 G6
Banbury Clo. SN3	22 B1	Berkeley Rd. SN4	20 D5	Bourton Av. SN3	10 D6
Bancroft Clo. SN5	12 B4	Berkshire Dr. SN5	12 C3	Bouverie Av. SN3	21 F1
Bankfoot Clo. SN5	12 D3	Berricot La. SN4	23 G6	Bow Ct. SN1	15 E6
Bankside SN1	14 B6	Berrington Rd. SN3	22 C1	Eastcott Rd.	
Banwell Av. SN3	16 C5	Berry Copse SN5	12 B1	Bowerfield SN3	23 F1
Barbury Clo. SN2	8 B5	Russley Clo.		Bowleymead SN3	17 F4
Barcelona Cres. SN4	20 C5	Berwick Way SN2	9 E4	Bowling Grn. La. SN1	21 E1
Barkstead Clo. SN5	12 D6	Inglesham Rd.		Bowman Clo. SN3	10 D5
Barnard Clo. SN3	16 D3	Bess Rd. SN5	12 B6	Bowood Rd. SN1	14 C6
Barnfield Clo. SN2	14 B3	Bessemer Clo. SN2	14 C1	Boydell Clo. SN5	12 D2
Barnfield Rd. SN2	13 G3	Bessemer Rd. E. SN2	14 C1	Bradenham Rd. SN5	12 C5
Barnmoor Clo. SN3	23 G1	Bessemer Rd. W. SN2	14 B1	Bradford Rd. SN1	15 E6
Barnstaple Clo. SN3	16 D5	Betony Clo. SN2	7 G3	Bradley Rd. SN2	9 F4
Barnum Ct. SN2	**24 A1**	Bevan Clo. SN2	10 B5	Bradwell Moor SN3	23 F2
Baron Clo. SN3	10 D5	Beverley SN5	13 E6	Braemar Clo. SN3	22 B1
Barrett Way SN4	20 C6	Beverstone Gro. SN3	16 B6	Bramble Clo. SN2	15 G1
Barrington Clo. SN3	23 F1	Bevil SN5	18 C1	Bramble Rd. SN2	15 G1
Barrowby Gate SN3	10 C4	Bevisland SN3	23 E1	Bramptons, The SN5	12 D3
Barry Glen Clo. SN2	15 G1	Bibury Rd. SN3	15 G5	Bramwell Clo. SN2	9 G2
Barton Rd. SN2	7 G5	Bideford Clo. SN3	16 C5	Brandon Clo. SN5	12 C5
Basil Clo. SN2	7 F4	Bindon Clo. SN5	12 B5	Branksome Rd. SN2	7 G5
Basingstoke Clo. SN5	12 C6	**Birch St. SN1**	**24 A5**	Bratton Clo. SN2	8 D3
Baskerville Rd. SN3	17 G3	Birches, The SN3	22 C2	Braybrooke Clo. SN5	12 B2
Bath Rd. SN1	14 D6	Birchwood Rd. SN3	10 D6	Sandacre Rd.	
Bathampton St. SN1	**24 B4**	Birdbrook Rd. SN2	9 G3	Braydon Ct. SN2	9 E3
Bathurst Rd. SN1	**25 G3**	Birdcombe Rd. SN5	13 E5	Penhill Dr.	
Bay Tree Ct. SN2	8 D6	Bishopdale Clo. SN5	12 C1	Brecon Clo. SN3	21 G2
Baydon Clo. SN2	8 B5	Bisley Clo. SN3	16 C5	Bremhill Clo. SN2	9 E4
Bayleaf Av. SN2	7 F4	Bittern Rd. SN3	17 G4	Brendon Wk. SN3	16 D4
Beales, The SN1	**24 D2**	Blackmore Clo. SN3	17 G3	Brettingham Gate	22 B4
Beatrice St. SN2	15 E2	Blackstone Av. SN3	17 E6	SN3	
Beatty Ct. SN3	15 F6	Bladen Clo. SN4	20 B6	Briar Flds. SN1	15 G2
Dammas La.		Blagrove SN5	18 C2	Briarswood Ct. SN3	23 F1
Beaufort Grn. SN3	16 D5	Blair Par. SN2	8 B5	Grundys	
Beaufort Rd. SN4	20 C5	Moredon Rd.		Bridge End Rd. SN3	16 B1
Beaulieu Clo. SN5	13 E6	Blake Cres. SN3	11 E6	**Bridge St. SN1**	**24 D3**
Beaumaris Rd. SN5	12 D5	Blakeney Av. SN3	16 D3	Bridgeman Clo. SN3	10 D6
Beaumont Rd. SN3	15 G4	Blakesley Clo. SN3	16 B6	Bridgemead Clo. SN5	13 F3
Beckhampton St. SN1	**25 F4**	Blandford Ct. SN3	16 D4	**Bridgewater Clo. SN2**	**24 A1**
Beddington Ct. SN3	10 C3	Blenheim Rd. SN4	20 C5	Bridport Rd. SN3	16 D6
Bedford Rd. SN3	15 G4	Bletchley Clo. SN3	17 E6	Briery Clo. SN3	10 C4
Lennox Dr.		Blockley Ri. SN3	10 C3	Bright St. SN2	15 F2
Bedwyn Clo. SN2	9 E5	Bloomsbury Clo. SN5	12 C6	Brimble Hill SN4	20 D6
Beech Av. SN2	8 C6	Bluebell Path SN2	7 G3	Brind Clo. SN3	17 G4
Beechcroft Rd. SN2	9 F5	Westfield Way		Brindley Clo. SN2	13 F1
Beehive Clo. SN5	12 C2	Blunsdon Rd. SN2	8 B4	Brington Rd. SN3	16 D2
Belgrave St. SN1	**25 F5**	Bodiam Dr. SN5	19 E1	**Bristol St. SN1**	**24 B4**
Bell Gdns. SN3	11 G4	Bodmin Clo. SN3	16 C5	Britannia Pl. SN1	15 F6
Belle Vue Rd. SN1	**25 G6**	Boldrewood SN3	23 F1	Brixham Av. SN3	15 G5
Bellver SN5	12 D5	Boleyn Clo. SN5	12 C4	**Broad St. SN1**	**25 F2**
Belmont Clo. SN3	10 C4	Bolingbroke Rd. SN2	7 G6	Broadmead Wk. SN3	16 D3
Belmont Cres. SN1	20 D1	Boness Rd. SN4	20 C5	Broadmoor Rd. SN3	11 F1
Belsay SN5	13 E6	Bonner Clo. SN5	12 B5	Broadway SN2	8 C5
Belvedere Rd. SN3	22 C1	Borage Clo. SN2	7 F3	Bromley Clo. SN3	15 G4
Bembridge Clo. SN3	16 D5	Boscombe Rd. SN2	7 G4	Bronte Clo. SN3	17 F6
Bentley Clo. SN3	16 C4	Bosham Clo. SN5	12 D6	Brookdene SN2	7 G4

Brookdene Lo. SN2	7	G4
Brookdene		
Brooklands Av. SN2	14	B1
Brooklime Clo. SN2	7	F4
Brooks Clo. SN2	9	G3
Brooksby Way SN3	16	D2
Broome Manor La. SN3	21	G2
Broughton Gra. SN3	16	B6
Brow, The SN2	7	G4
Browning Clo. SN3	10	D5
Bruce St. SN2	14	B3
Bruddel Gro. SN3	21	G2
Brunel Plaza SN1	14	D4
Brunel Shopping Cen.		
Brunel Shopping Cen. SN1	**24**	**D4**
Brunswick St. SN1	15	E6
Bruton Wk. SN3	16	C5
Whitbourne Av.		
Bryanston Way SN3	17	E4
Bryony Way SN2	7	F4
Buckhurst Cres. SN3	16	C4
Buckingham Rd. SN3	22	B1
Buckland Clo. SN3	16	D4
Bucklebury Clo. SN3	16	C1
Buckthorn Dr. SN2	7	F4
Buie Clo. SN5	6	D6
Buller St. SN2	15	F1
Bullfinch Clo. SN3	17	F4
Bunce Rd. SN3	10	C6
Bungalows, The SN2	8	D6
Buntings, The SN3	17	F3
Burbage Rd. SN2	9	E2
Burden Clo. SN3	17	E1
Burderop Clo. SN4	20	D4
Burford Av. SN3	15	G5
Burgess Clo. SN3	16	C1
Burghley Clo. SN3	16	B4
Burnet Clo. SN2	7	F3
Burnham Rd. SN3	16	D4
Burns Way SN2	9	G4
Buttermere SN3	23	F1
Butterworth St. SN1	**24**	**A5**
Byfield Way SN3	16	D2
Byrd Clo. SN5	12	B5
Byron Ct. SN3	11	G3
Byron St. SN1	**25**	**F5**
C		
Cabot Dr. SN5	12	B4
Cadley Clo. SN2	9	E6
Caernarvon Wk. SN3	22	B2
Sandringham Rd.		
Cairndow Way SN2	9	G3
Calder Clo. SN2	8	B3
Callaghan Clo. SN3	10	C6
Midwinter Gdns.		
Calvert Rd. SN3	15	G4
Cambria Bri. Rd. SN1	**24**	**B5**
Cambria Pl. SN1	**24**	**B5**
Cambridge Clo. SN3	22	B1
Camden Clo. SN5	12	C5
Cameron Clo. SN3	16	C1
Campden Rd. SN3	15	G5
Campion Gate SN5	12	B5
Camton Rd. SN5	12	B3
Canal Wk. SN1	**24**	**D4**
Canford Clo. SN3	17	E4
Cannon St. SN1	**25**	**F6**
Canterbury Clo. SN3	22	B1
Capitol Clo. SN3	17	F1
Caprice Clo. SN5	12	C3
Caraway Dr. SN2	7	E4
Cardigan Clo. SN3	16	B6
Cardwell Clo. SN3	16	D3
Carey Clo. SN5	12	C5
Carfax St. SN1	**25**	**E2**
Carlisle Av. SN3	21	F1
Carlton Gate SN3	22	B3
Carman Clo. SN3	10	D5
Carr St. SN1	**24**	**D3**
Carroll Clo. SN3	17	F6
Carronbridge Rd. SN5	12	D4
Carshalton Rd. SN3	22	D1
Carstairs Av. SN3	22	C1
Cartwright Dr. SN5	12	C2
Casson Rd. SN3	10	C6
Castle Dore SN5	12	C5
Castle Vw. Rd. SN3	17	E1
Castlefield Clo. SN5	12	D4
Castleton Rd. SN5	12	B3
Catherine St. SN1	14	D4
Fleet St.		
Catherine Wayte Clo. SN2	8	B4
Catmint Clo. SN2	7	F4
Caulfield Rd. SN2	15	F2
Cavendish Sq. SN3	16	C6
Kingston Rd.		
Caversham Clo. SN3	16	B5
Cavie Clo. SN5	12	C2
Caxton Clo. SN3	16	B6
Cayenne Pk. SN2	7	E4
Cecil Rd. SN3	16	C4
Cedars Clo. SN2	8	C6
Centurion Way SN3	17	E2
Chalford Av. SN3	16	D3
Chalgrove Fld. SN5	18	C1
Gainsborough Way		
Chamberlain Rd. SN3	10	C6
Chancellor Clo. SN5	12	B4
Chandler Clo. SN1	**25**	**G6**
Chandos Clo. SN5	12	C4
Chantry Rd. SN2	8	B5
Chapel La. SN3	11	G3
Chapel St. SN2	15	F2
Charfield Clo. SN3	16	C6
Charlbury Clo. SN2	8	B5
Charles McPhearson Gdns. SN3	17	E5
Charlock Path SN2	7	G3
Windflower Rd.		
Charlotte Ms. SN1	15	F6
Charlton Clo. SN2	9	F3
Charminster Clo. SN3	17	E4
Charolais Dr. SN5	12	C3
Charterhouse Rd. SN4	20	C6
Maskeleyne Way		
Chartley Grn. SN5	12	C5
Chase Wd. SN5	6	C6
Chatsworth Rd. SN2	8	B3
Cheddar Rd. SN2	7	G5
Chedworth Gate SN3	22	B3
Chelmsford Rd. SN5	13	E3
Cheltenham St. SN1	**24**	**D2**
Cheney Manor Ind. Est. SN2	13	G1
Cheney Manor Rd. SN2	8	C5
Chepstow Clo. SN5	19	E1
Cheraton Clo. SN3	16	D3
Cherbury Wk. SN3	16	C4
Courtenay Rd.		
Cherhill Ct. SN2	7	G5
Abbey Vw. Rd.		
Cherry Tree Gro. SN2	9	E6
Chervil Rd. SN2	7	E4
Chesford Clo. SN3	22	C1
Chester St. SN1	**24**	**C4**
Chesterfield Clo. SN5	13	E4
Silchester Way		
Chesters, The SN5	13	E4
Chestnut Av. SN2	9	E5
Chevalier Clo. SN5	12	B2
Cheviot Clo. SN5	12	C4
Chickerell Rd. SN3	16	C5
Chicory Clo. SN2	7	E5
Chilton Gdns. SN2	8	B5
Fernham Rd.		
Chippenham Clo. SN2	8	D2
Chippenham Wk. SN2	8	D2
Ramsbury Av.		
Chives Way SN2	7	F4
Chobham Clo. SN3	10	C3
Beddington Ct.		
Christie Clo. SN3	17	F6
Chudleigh SN5	12	D6
Church Pl. SN1	**24**	**A4**
Church Rd. SN1	15	F6
Church St. SN3	10	D6
Church Wk. SN2	10	B5
Church Wk. N. SN2	8	B5
Church Wk. S. SN2	8	B5
Church Way SN3	10	C6
Churchfield SN2	8	B4
Churchward Av. SN2	14	C1
Circle, The SN2	9	E5
Cirencester Ct. SN1	15	F5
Drove Rd.		

Dudley Rd. SN3	16 B4	Ely Clo. SN5	13 E6	**Fleming Way SN1**	**24 D3**
Dudmore Rd. SN3	**25 H3**	**Emlyn Sq. SN1**	**24 C3**	Flint Hill SN5	13 E6
Duke's Clo. SN2	9 G3	Emmanuel Clo. SN2	8 C4	Florence St. SN2	15 E2
Dulverton Av. SN3	16 C5	Enford Av. SN2	9 E2	Folkstone Rd. SN1	14 D6
Dumbarton Ter. SN1	**25 F6**	Eric Long Ct. SN3	17 F6	Fonthill Wk. SN3	15 G5
Dunbar Rd. SN4	20 C5	Erlestoke Way SN2	9 E2	*Eastern Av.*	
Dunbeath Ct. SN2	15 G1	*Westwood Rd.*		**Ford St. SN1**	**24 A5**
Dunbeath Rd. SN2	15 G1	Ermin St. SN2	10 B3	Forester Clo. SN3	17 F6
Dunbeath Trd. Est.	15 G1	Ermin St. SN3	10 D5	Forsey Clo. SN3	17 G3
SN2		Eshton Wk. SN3	22 C1	Forum, The SN5	13 E5
Dunraven Clo. SN3	16 B6	*Queens Dr.*		*Rivenhall Rd.*	
Dunsford Clo. SN1	14 B6	Espringham Pl. SN2	9 G4	Forum Clo. SN3	17 E2
Dunster Clo. SN3	21 G1	*Brooks Clo.*		Fosse Clo. SN2	14 B4
Dunwich Dr. SN5	13 F6	Essex Wk. SN3	16 B4	Fowey SN5	18 C1
Durham St. SN1	**25 F5**	**Euclid St. SN1**	**25 F4**	Fox, The SN5	6 B5
Durnford Rd. SN2	9 E3	Europa Ind. Pk. SN3	10 B5	Fox Wd. SN5	13 F5
Durrington Wk. SN2	9 E3	Euroway SN5	18 B2	Foxbridge SN3	17 F3
Penhill Dr.		Evelyn St. SN3	21 F1	Foxglove Rd. SN2	7 F3
		Evergreens Clo. SN3	17 E1	Foxhill Clo. SN2	8 B5
E		Everleigh Rd. SN2	9 E3	Foxley Clo. SN2	9 G4
Eagle Clo. SN3	17 G3	Eworth Clo. SN5	12 B5	Frampton Clo. SN5	12 D4
Sandpiper Bri.		Exe Clo. SN2	8 C4	Francomes SN2	7 G4
Earl Clo. SN5	12 B3	**Exeter St. SN1**	**24 B4**	Frankland Rd. SN5	18 B2
East St. SN1	**24 C3**	**Exmouth St. SN1**	**24 B6**	Frankton Gdns. SN3	10 D6
Eastcott Hill SN1	**25 E6**			Fraser Clo. SN3	16 D3
Eastcott Rd. SN1	15 E6	**F**		Freshbrook Way SN5	12 D6
Eastern Av. SN3	15 G4	Fairfax Clo. SN3	16 B3	Fresian Clo. SN5	12 C3
Eastleaze Rd. SN5	13 E4	Fairford Cres. SN2	9 E5	Friesland Clo. SN5	12 C3
Eastmere SN3	23 G1	Fairholme Way SN2	10 B4	*Saddleback Rd.*	
Eastville Rd. SN2	9 E5	Fairlawn SN3	23 E1	Frilford Dr. SN3	16 C1
Eaton Clo. SN3	22 C1	**Fairview SN1**	**24 C6**	Frobisher Dr. SN3	16 B3
Eaton Wd. SN5	6 C6	Falconscroft SN3	17 E2	Frome Rd. SN2	8 B4
Eccleston Clo. SN3	22 D1	Falkirk Rd. SN4	20 C5	Fuller Clo. SN2	10 B3
Ecklington SN3	17 E5	Falmouth Gro. SN3	15 G6	Furlong Clo. SN2	7 G3
Edale Moor SN3	23 G1	Fanstones Rd. SN3	17 E6	Furze Clo. SN5	6 C6
Edgar Row Clo. SN4	20 C6	Faraday Rd. SN3	17 G6	Fyfield Av. SN2	9 E3
Wharf Rd.		Fareham Clo. SN3	16 D5	Fyne Clo. SN5	6 D6
Edgehill SN5	18 D1	**Faringdon Rd. SN1**	**24 B5**	*Orrin Clo.*	
Edgeware Rd. SN1	**25 E4**	Farleigh Cres. SN3	21 G1		
Edgeworth Clo. SN5	12 D3	Farman Clo. SN3	17 E6	**G**	
Edinburgh St. SN2	15 F1	Farnborough Rd. SN3	22 D1	Gainsborough Way	12 C5
Edington Clo. SN5	12 D5	**Farnsby St. SN1**	**24 C4**	SN5	
Edison Rd. SN3	17 F5	Farrfield SN2	9 G4	Gairlock Clo. SN5	6 D6
Edmund St. SN1	**25 E5**	Farriers Clo. SN1	15 G2	Galloway Clo. SN5	12 C3
Egerton Clo. SN3	16 D3	Feather Wd. SN5	13 F5	*Tamworth Dr.*	
Elborough Rd. SN2	7 F5	Fenland Clo. SN5	12 B2	Galsworthy Clo. SN3	17 F6
Elcombe Av. SN4	20 B6	Fennel Clo. SN2	7 F4	**Gambia St. SN1**	**25 H3**
Eldene Dr. SN3	17 E5	Ferndale Rd. SN2	14 B2	Gantlettdene SN3	17 G4
Elder Clo. SN2	7 E5	Fernham Rd. SN2	8 B5	Ganton Way SN2	15 G1
Elgin Dr. SN2	15 G1	Ferns, The SN2	15 E2	Garfield Clo. SN3	23 E1
Elgin Ind. Est. SN2	15 F1	Ferrers Dr. SN5	12 B6	Garrard Way SN3	16 C2
Eliot Clo. SN3	23 F1	Field Ri. SN1	20 C1	Gartons Rd. SN5	12 B3
Grundys		Fieldfare SN3	17 F3	Gay's Pl. SN2	10 B4
Ellingdon Rd. SN4	20 B5	Finchdale SN3	17 F2	Gayton Way SN3	16 D2
Elm Gro. SN5	12 C2	Fir Tree Clo. SN2	8 C6	**George St. SN1**	**24 A5**
Elmina Rd. SN1	**25 F1**	Firth Clo. SN2	8 C5	Gerard Wk. SN5	12 C4
Elmore SN3	17 E5	Fitzmaurice Clo. SN3	17 F3	Gibbs Clo. SN3	17 G3
Elms, The SN5	12 B2	Fitzroy Rd. SN1	21 E2	Gifford Rd. SN3	10 D5
Elmswood Clo. SN2	9 G3	**Fleet St. SN1**	**24 D3**	Gilling Way SN3	17 F4
Elsham Way SN2	8 B3	Fleetwood Ct. SN5	18 C1	Gipsy La. SN2	15 G2

Gladstone St. **SN1**	25	**F1**
Gladys Plumley Gdns.	15	F2
SN2		
Hinton St.		
Glenwood Clo. SN1	21	E2
Glevum Rd. SN3	17	E1
Globe St. SN1	15	E6
Gloucester St. **SN1**	**24**	**D2**
Goddard Av. SN1	14	D6
Godolphin Clo. SN5	18	B1
Godwin Rd. SN3	10	D5
Goldcrest Wk. SN3	17	G3
Magpie La.		
Goldsborough Clo.	12	D4
SN5		
Gooch St. **SN1**	**25**	**F1**
Gordon Gdns. **SN1**	**25**	**E3**
Gordon Rd. **SN1**	**25**	**E3**
Goulding Clo. SN3	10	C6
Gower Clo. SN2	10	B6
Gower Clo. SN5	12	B5
Grafton Rd. SN2	9	E3
Graham St. **SN1**	**25**	**G1**
Grailey Clo. SN3	17	E6
Granary Clo. SN5	12	B2
Grandison Clo. SN5	12	B4
Grange Dr. SN3	16	C1
Grange Pk. Way SN5	12	B5
Grantham Clo. SN5	18	D1
Grantley Clo. SN3	22	C1
Granville St. **SN1**	**24**	**D5**
Grasmere SN3	23	G1
Great Western Way	14	C2
SN2		
Great Western Way	18	C1
SN5		
Green Meadow Av.	8	B4
SN2		
Green Rd. SN2	9	G5
Green Valley Av. SN2	8	B4
Greenbridge Ind. Est.	16	C2
SN3		
Greenbridge Rd. SN3	16	C3
Greenfields SN3	11	G3
Greenhill Rd. SN2	7	G6
Greenlands Rd. SN2	9	G5
Greenway Clo. SN3	16	D3
Gresham Clo. SN3	16	B4
Greywethers Av.	21	G1
SN3		
Griffiths Clo. SN3	16	D1
Grindal Dr. SN5	12	B5
Grosmont Dr. SN5	12	D5
Grosvenor Rd. SN1	14	C6
Groundwell Ind. Est.	9	F2
SN2		
Groundwell Rd. **SN1**	**25**	**F5**
Grove St. SN2	14	B4
Grovelands Av. SN1	21	E1
Grundys SN3	23	F1

Guildford Av. SN3	22	B1
Guppy St. SN2	14	B4

H

Hackett Clo. SN2	9	G3
Hackleton Ri. SN3	16	D2
Hackpen Clo. SN4	20	D4
Haddon Clo. SN5	12	B5
Hadleigh Clo. SN5	13	E4
Hadleigh Ri. SN3	10	C3
Hadrians Clo. SN3	17	E1
Haig Clo. SN2	9	G4
Halifax Clo. SN4	20	C5
Hall Clo. SN4	20	C6
Hallam Moor SN3	23	G2
Hamble Rd. SN2	8	B4
Hamilton Clo. SN3	16	B3
Hampshire Clo. SN5	12	C3
Berkshire Dr.		
Hampton Dr. SN5	12	B4
Hamworthy Rd. SN3	17	E4
Hanbury Rd. SN3	16	B6
Handel St. SN2	15	E2
Hannington Clo. SN2	8	D2
Hanson Clo. SN5	12	D2
Harbour Clo. SN2	8	B5
Harcourt Rd. SN2	14	C2
Hardie Clo. SN3	10	C6
Harding St. **SN1**	**24**	**C3**
Hardwick Clo. SN2	8	B3
Harebell Clo. SN2	7	F3
Hargreaves Rd. SN2	9	F2
Harlech Clo. SN5	12	D6
Harlestone Rd. SN3	16	D2
Harptree Clo. SN5	12	C2
Harriers, The SN3	17	E3
Harrington Wk. SN3	16	B3
Frobisher Dr.		
Harris Rd. SN2	8	C6
Harrow Clo. SN3	16	B1
Hartland Clo. SN3	16	C5
Hartsthorn Clo. SN2	7	F5
Harvester Clo. SN5	12	B2
Harvey Gro. SN2	8	B6
Hathaway Rd. SN2	9	G3
Hatherall Clo. SN3	11	E6
Hatherleigh Ct. SN3	16	D4
Marlowe Av.		
Hatherley Rd. SN3	16	D3
Hathersage Moor	23	G2
SN3		
Hatton Gro. SN3	16	B4
Havelock Sq. SN1	14	D4
Brunel Shopping Cen.		
Havelock St. **SN1**	**24**	**D4**
Haven Clo. SN3	16	D2
Hawfinch Clo. SN3	17	G5
Hawker Rd. SN3	17	E6
Hawkins St. SN2	14	B3
Hawkswood SN3	17	F2

Hawksworth Way	**24**	**B1**
SN2		
Hawthorn Av. SN2	9	E6
Hay La. SN5	12	B3
Haydon Ct. SN2	7	G3
Haydon Ct. Dr. SN2	7	G3
Haydon End La. SN2	7	G2
Haydon St. **SN1**	**25**	**E2**
Haydon Vw. Rd. SN2	9	E4
Haydonleigh Dr. SN2	7	G4
Haynes Clo. SN3	17	E6
Fanstones Rd.		
Hazel Gro. SN2	9	E5
Hazelbury Cres. SN3	17	E3
Hazlemere Clo. SN3	16	D6
Headlands Gro. SN2	9	F5
Headlands Trd. Est.	9	G5
SN2		
Heath Way SN3	16	D2
Slade Dr.		
Heathcote Clo. SN5	12	D2
Heaton Clo. SN2	8	C2
Heddington Clo. SN2	8	D3
Hedges Clo. SN3	10	D5
Shenton Clo.		
Heights, The SN1	14	C6
Helmsdale SN2	8	B4
Helmsdale Wk. SN3	16	C6
Belvedere Rd.		
Helston Rd. SN3	16	C5
Henley Rd. SN3	16	B6
Henry St. **SN1**	**24**	**D3**
Hereford Lawns SN3	22	B1
Hermitage La. SN2	9	G5
Heronbridge Clo. SN5	13	E5
Heronscroft SN3	17	F2
Hertford Clo. SN3	16	B4
Hesketh Cres. SN3	21	F1
Hewitt Clo. SN3	17	E6
Hexham Clo. SN5	12	D5
Heytsbury Gdns. SN5	12	B6
Heywood Clo. SN2	8	D3
Hicks Clo. SN4	20	C6
High St. SN1	15	F6
High St. SN2	7	G4
Highclere Av. SN3	16	B6
Highdown Way SN2	8	C1
Highland Clo. SN5	12	C3
Berkshire Dr.		
Highmoor Copse SN5	12	C1
Swinley Dr.		
Highnam Clo. SN3	16	C1
Highwood Clo. SN2	7	F4
Highworth Rd. SN3	10	D3
Highworth Rd.	11	G2
(South Marston) SN3		
Hill Vw. Rd. SN3	17	E1
Hillary Clo. SN2	9	E4
Hillingdon Rd. SN3	16	D6
Hillmarton Av. SN2	9	E3

Hillmead Dr. SN5	12 D1	Isis Clo. SN2	8 C5	King Henry Dr. SN5	12 B6
Hillmead Ind. Est. SN5	12 D2	Isis Trd. Est. SN1	16 B2	King John St. SN1	15 F6
		Islandsmead SN3	17 E5	*Victoria Rd.*	
Hillside Av. SN1	14 C6	Islington St. SN1	**25 E3**	**King St. SN1**	**24 D3**
Hillyard Clo. SN5	12 B6	Ixworth Clo. SN5	12 C3	King William St. SN1	15 E6
Hinton St. SN2	15 F2			Kingfisher Dr. SN3	17 F3
Hobley Dr. SN3	10 C5	**J**		Kingscote Clo. SN5	12 B2
Holbein Clo. SN5	12 C5	Jacobs Wk. SN3	17 F6	Kingsdown Caravan Pk. SN2	10 C2
Holbein Ct. SN5	12 C5	**James Watt Clo. SN2**	**24 B2**		
Holbein Fld. SN5	12 C5	Jasmine Clo. SN2	7 F4	Kingsdown Rd. SN2	10 B3
Holbein Ms. SN5	12 C5	Jefferies Av. SN2	9 F6	Kingsdown Rd. SN3	10 C2
Holbein Pl. SN5	12 C5	Jennings St. SN2	14 B4	Kingshill Rd. SN1	14 C6
Holbein Sq. SN5	12 C6	Jersey Pk. SN5	12 D2	Kingsley Way SN2	9 F3
Holbrook Way SN1	**24 D3**	Jewel Clo. SN5	12 B5	Kingsthorpe Gro. SN3	17 E2
Holinshead Pl. SN5	12 C5	John Herring Cres. SN3	16 C1	Kingston Rd. SN3	16 C6
Holland Wk. SN3	15 G4			Kingsway Clo. SN3	16 B6
Lennox Dr.		**John St. SN1**	**24 D3**	Kingswood Av. SN3	16 C5
Hollins Moor SN3	23 F2	**Jolliffe St. SN1**	**24 A5**	Kipling Gdns. SN2	9 G4
Holly Clo. SN2	8 C6	**Joseph St. SN1**	**24 B5**	Kirby Clo. SN3	16 B6
Holmleigh SN2	7 G4	Jubilee Rd. SN2	7 F5	Kirkstall Clo. SN5	13 E6
Honeybone Wk. SN3	17 G3	Juliana Clo. SN5	12 C3	Kirktonhill Rd. SN5	13 F4
Cornmarsh Way		Juniper Clo. SN3	16 D2	Kishorn Clo. SN5	6 D6
Honeysuckle Clo. SN2	7 F3			Kitchener St. SN2	15 E1
Cornflower Rd.		**K**		Knapp Clo. SN2	8 B6
Honiton Rd. SN3	16 D5	Karslake Clo. SN3	17 E6	Knoll, The SN1	21 E1
Hook St. SN5	12 A5	Keats Cres. SN2	10 B4	Knolton Wk. SN3	16 C6
Hooper Pl. SN1	15 F6	Kelham Clo. SN3	16 B6	*Priory Rd.*	
Hopton Clo. SN5	18 D1	Kellsboro Rd. SN4	20 B5	Knowsley Rd. SN3	16 C6
Horace St. SN2	14 B3	Kelmscot Rd. SN2	9 E5		
Hornbeam Ct. SN2	8 D6	Kelvin Rd. SN3	16 C3	**L**	
Hornsey Gdns. SN3	10 C3	**Kemble Dr. SN2**	**24 A2**	Laburnum Rd. SN2	9 E5
Horseshoe Cres. SN5	12 C1	Kembrey Pk. SN2	9 G6	Lacock Rd. SN2	9 E4
Horsham Cres. SN3	16 C6	Kembrey St. SN2	9 F6	Lady La. SN2	8 B2
Howard Clo. SN3	16 B4	Kemerton Wk. SN3	22 D1	**Lagos St. SN1**	**25 F2**
Hughes St. SN2	13 G3	*Denholme Rd.*		Lakeside SN3	21 G1
Hungerford Clo. SN5	12 B3	Kendal SN5	12 D6	Lambert Clo. SN5	18 D1
Spencer Clo.		Kenilworth Lawns SN3	22 B1	Lambourn Av. SN3	21 G1
Hunsdon Clo. SN3	16 C4			Lamora Clo. SN5	12 B2
Hunt St. SN1	**25 F6**	Kennedy Dr. SN3	17 F5	Lanac Rd. SN3	16 C1
Hunters Gro. SN2	14 D1	Kennet Av. SN2	8 D4	Lancaster Rd. SN4	20 C6
Huntley Clo. SN3	16 B3	Kennet Rd. SN4	20 C5	Langdale Dr. SN5	18 D1
Hunts Ri. SN3	11 E2	**Kent Rd. SN1**	**24 D6**	Langford Gro. SN3	15 G4
Hurst Cres. SN2	9 E5	Kenton Clo. SN3	16 D4	Langport Clo. SN5	12 C6
Hyde, The SN5	6 A4	Kenwin Clo. SN3	10 D5	*Gainsborough Way*	
Hyde Rd. SN2	9 G2	Kerrs Way SN4	20 C6	Langstone Way SN5	13 E4
Hylder Clo. SN2	7 F4	Kerry Clo. SN5	12 C3	Lanhydrock Clo. SN5	12 C6
Hysopp Clo. SN2	7 E4	Kershaw Rd. SN3	17 E6	Lansbury Dr. SN2	10 B4
Southernwood Dr.		Kestrel Dr. SN3	17 G4	Lansdown Rd. SN1	14 D6
Hythe Rd. SN1	**24 D6**	Keswick Rd. SN3	22 D1	Lapwing Clo. SN3	17 G4
		Keycroft Copse SN5	12 B1	Larchmore Clo. SN2	8 C5
I		Keyneston Rd. SN3	17 E4	Larksfield SN3	17 E2
Icomb Clo. SN5	13 E6	Keynsham Wk. SN3	16 D6	Lawrence Clo. SN3	17 E6
Idovers Dr. SN5	13 E6	Kilben Clo. SN5	12 B3	Lawton Clo. SN3	22 C1
Iffley Rd. SN2	14 B2	Kiln La. SN2	14 B1	Layton Clo. SN2	8 D2
Imber Wk. SN2	8 D2	Kilsby Dr. SN3	16 D2	Lea Clo. SN2	8 C1
Ramsbury Av.		Kilsyth Clo. SN5	12 C5	Leamington Gro. SN3	21 G2
Inglesham Rd. SN2	9 E4	Kimberley Rd. SN3	16 B6	**Leicester St. SN1**	**25 G4**
Inverary Rd. SN4	20 C5	Kimbolton Clo. SN5	12 C6	Leigh Rd. SN2	9 E4
Ipswich St. SN2	15 E2	Kimmeridge Clo. SN3	16 D4	Leighton Av. SN3	16 B6
Irston Way SN5	12 D6	King Charles Rd. SN5	12 D6	Lennox Dr. SN3	15 G4

Morrison St. SN2	14	B3	Ocotal Way SN1	15	F2	Penfold Gdns. SN1	15	E6
Morse St. SN1	**24**	**D5**	Odstock Rd. SN2	9	E2	Penhill Dr. SN2	8	D3
Mortimer Clo. SN5	12	D3	Okebourne Pk. SN3	23	E1	Penny La. SN3	16	B3
Mountings, The SN4	20	D4	Okeford Clo. SN3	17	E3	Pennycress Clo. SN2	7	G4
Mulberry Gro. SN2	8	C6	Okus Gro. SN2	9	F4	Penrose Wk. SN3	16	C5
Mulcaster Av. SN5	12	B5	Okus Rd. SN1	14	C6	*Banwell Av.*		
Mundy Av. SN3	17	E6	Old Mill La. SN3	21	F1	Pentridge Clo. SN3	17	E3
Murdoch Rd. SN3	17	G4	Old Shaw La. SN5	12	C2	Penzance Dr. SN5	13	G5
Myrtle Gdns. SN2	9	E6	Oldlands Wk. SN3	22	D1	Percheron Clo. SN5	12	C3
			Olive Gro. SN2	8	D5	Percy St. SN2	14	B3
N			Oliver Clo. SN5	12	B4	Peregrine Clo. SN3	17	F2
Nantwich SN5	18	C1	Omdurman St. SN2	14	D1	Periwinkle Clo. SN2	7	E5
Napier Clo. SN2	**24**	**A1**	Orchard Gro. SN2	9	F5	Perry's La. SN4	20	C6
Naunton Rd. SN3	16	C4	Orchid Clo. SN2	9	E5	Peter Furkins Ct. SN1	14	C5
Nelson St. SN1	14	B5	Orkney Clo. SN5	12	D3	*Westcott Pl.*		
Ness Clo. SN5	6	D6	Orlando Clo. SN5	12	B5	Petersfield Rd. SN3	16	D6
Gairlock Clo.			Orrin Clo. SN5	12	D1	Petter Clo. SN4	20	D4
Netherton Clo. SN3	16	D6	Orwell Clo. SN2	8	C3	Pevensey Way SN5	12	D5
Nevis Clo. SN5	6	D6	Osborne St. SN2	14	D2	Pewsham Rd. SN2	9	F3
New Bri. Sq. SN1	**25**	**E2**	Osprey Clo. SN3	17	G4	Pheasant Clo. SN3	17	G4
New Meadow Copse	12	C1	Osterley Rd. SN2	7	G2	Pickwick Clo. SN2	9	G3
SN5			Overbrook SN3	16	D6	Picton Rd. SN5	12	C3
Newark Clo. SN5	18	D1	Overton Gdns. SN3	10	D6	Pigeon Ho. La. SN3	10	C5
Newburn Cres. SN1	14	B5	Owl Clo. SN3	17	G4	Pilgrim Clo. SN5	12	C3
Newbury Dr. SN5	18	D1	Owlets, The SN3	17	G3	Pilton Clo. SN5	12	B2
Newcastle St. SN1	**25**	**G4**	*Sandpiper Bri.*			Pinehurst Rd. SN2	14	D1
Newcome Dr. SN2	14	C3	Oxford Rd. SN3	16	C1	Pinetree Ri. SN2	8	D5
Newhall St. SN1	**24**	**D5**	**Oxford St. SN1**	**24**	**C3**	Pinnegar Way SN3	17	G4
Newland Rd. SN2	8	C5				Pinnock's Pl. SN2	10	B4
Newport St. SN1	21	F1	**P**			Pioneer Clo. SN5	12	C3
Newton Way SN2	9	E4	Paddington Dr. SN5	13	G4	*Majestic Clo.*		
Nightingale La. SN3	11	H4	Paddock Clo. SN2	7	G3	Pipers Way SN3	21	F2
Nindum Rd. SN3	16	D1	Paddocks, The SN3	10	C6	Pipitdene SN3	17	F3
Norcliffe Rd. SN3	16	D6	Pakenham Rd. SN3	16	D6	Planks, The SN3	15	F6
Norfolk Clo. SN3	16	B4	**Parade, The SN1**	**24**	**D3**	Plattes Clo. SN5	12	D2
Norman Rd. SN2	15	E2	Parham Wk. SN5	12	B5	Pleydell Rd. SN1	21	E2
North Leaze Clo. SN2	8	B5	**Park La. SN1**	**24**	**A4**	Plummer Clo. SN4	20	C6
North Star Av. SN2	14	D2	Park Springs SN5	13	E5	**Plymouth St. SN1**	**25**	**G3**
North St. SN1	**25**	**E6**	Park St. SN3	11	E6	Poltondale SN3	17	F3
Northampton St. SN1	**25**	**G4**	**Parklands Rd. SN3**	**25**	**H6**	Pond St. SN2	8	B3
Northbrook Rd. SN2	14	C1	Parkside SN3	10	C5	**Ponting St. SN1**	**25**	**F1**
Northern Rd. SN2	8	C6	Parkstone Wk. SN3	22	D1	Poole Rd. SN2	7	G5
Northfield Way SN3	16	D3	*Cranmore Av.*			Poplar Av. SN2	9	E6
Norton Gro. SN3	**25**	**H5**	Parr Clo. SN5	12	C4	Popplechurch Dr. SN3	17	G3
Norwood Clo. SN3	17	F6	Parsley Clo. SN2	7	F3	Portal Rd. SN2	8	C6
Nuffield Clo. SN5	13	E2	Parsonage Rd. SN3	10	C5	Portland Av. SN1	14	C6
Nuthatch Clo. SN3	17	G4	Partridge Clo. SN3	17	G4	Portmore Clo. SN5	7	E6
Nutmeg Clo. SN2	7	F4	Passmore Clo. SN3	17	G3	**Portsmouth St. SN1**	**25**	**G3**
Nyland Rd. SN3	17	E3	Pasture Clo. SN2	13	G3	Potterdown Rd. SN2	9	E3
Nythe Rd. SN3	16	D1	Patney Wk. SN2	8	D2	Poulton St. SN2	15	E2
			Hannington Clo.			Pound La. SN2	8	D6
O			Paulet Clo. SN5	12	B6	Poynings Way SN5	12	B6
Oak Gdn. SN3	10	C4	*Lumley Clo.*			Primrose Clo. SN2	7	F3
Oak Tree Av. SN2	9	F5	Pearce Clo. SN2	9	G2	**Princes St. SN1**	**25**	**F3**
Oakford Wk. SN3	16	C4	Pearl Rd. SN5	12	B3	Priory Rd. SN3	16	C6
Kingswood Av.			Peatmoor Way SN5	12	C1	Pritchard Clo. SN2	10	B3
Oakham Clo. SN5	13	E6	Pembroke Gdns. SN2	7	G5	**Prospect Hill SN1**	**25**	**F6**
Oaksey Rd. SN2	9	E4	Pembroke St. SN1	15	E6	**Prospect Pl. SN1**	**25**	**F6**
Oakwood Rd. SN5	13	E3	Pen Clo. SN2	8	C4	Purbeck Clo. SN3	17	E3
Oasthouse Clo. SN5	12	C2	Pendennis Rd. SN5	18	C1	Purley Av. SN3	22	D1

Purley Rd. SN4	23	H3
Purslane Clo. SN2	7	E5
Purton Rd. SN2	6	D6
Purton Rd. SN5	6	C6

Q

Quarries, The SN1	21	E1
Quarry Ms. SN1	21	E1
Quarry Rd. SN1	15	E6
Quarrybrook Clo. SN3	11	G3
Queen St. SN1	24	D3
Queenborough SN5	13	E6
Queens Dr. SN3	15	G4
Queensfield SN2	9	F3
Quentin Rd. SN3	21	F1

R

Radcot Clo. SN5	12	C1
Radley Clo. SN3	17	E3
Radnor St. SN1	24	B6
Radstock Av. SN3	16	D4
Radway Rd. SN3	10	B5
Raggett St. SN1	25	E6
Raglan Clo. SN3	21	G2
Rainer Clo. SN3	10	D5
Raleigh Av. SN3	16	B4
Ramleaze Dr. SN5	12	C3
Ramsbury Av. SN2	8	D2
Ramsden Rd. SN5	18	B2
Ramsthorn Clo. SN2	7	F4
Randall Cres. SN5	12	C2
Randolph Clo. SN3	16	B5
Rannoch Clo. SN5	6	D6
Ransome Clo. SN5	12	D2
Ravenglass Rd. SN5	13	E4
Ravenscroft SN3	17	E2
Rawlings Clo. SN3	11	G4
Rawston Clo. SN3	17	E4
Ray Clo. SN2	8	C4
Raybrook Cres. SN2	13	G4
Rayfield Gro. SN2	14	D2
Read St. SN1	24	B5
Reading St. SN1	24	C3
Redcap Gdns. SN5	12	C3
Redcliffe St. SN2	14	B4
Redlynch Clo. SN2	9	E3
Redruth Clo. SN3	16	D5
Reeves Clo. SN3	17	E6
Hawker Rd.		
Regent Circ. SN1	25	E5
Regent St. SN1	24	D3
Retingham Way SN3	10	C3
Revell Clo. SN2	9	G4
Rhuddlan SN5	12	D6
Richmond Rd. SN2	14	C1
Ridge Grn. SN5	12	D3
Ridge Nether Moor SN3	23	G2
Ridgeway Clo. SN2	8	B6
Ridgeway Rd. SN2	9	G3

Ringwood Clo. SN3	16	D4
Rinsdale Clo. SN5	12	D1
Ripley Rd. SN1	15	E6
Ripon Way SN3	22	C1
Ripple Fld. SN5	12	D6
Risingham Mead SN5	13	E5
Rivenhall Rd. SN5	13	E5
Riverdale Clo. SN1	21	E2
Rivermead Dr. SN5	13	E2
Rivermead Ind. Est. SN5	13	E2
Robinsgreen SN3	17	F3
Robinson Clo. SN3	17	F4
Roche Clo. SN3	17	F6
Rochester Clo. SN5	12	D6
Rochford Clo. SN5	12	C5
Rockdown Ct. SN2	9	F4
Somerford Clo.		
Rodbourne Rd. SN2	14	B2
Rodwell Clo. SN3	16	C6
Wallsworth Rd.		
Rogers Clo. SN3	16	C3
Rolleston St. SN1	25	F5
Roman Cres. SN1	20	D1
Romney Way SN5	12	C4
Rose St. SN2	14	B3
Rosebery St. SN1	25	G1
Rosedale Rd. SN3	16	D6
Rosemary Clo. SN2	7	F3
Rosewood Ct. SN3	23	F1
Grundys		
Ross Gdns. SN3	10	C4
Rother Clo. SN2	8	B3
Roughmoor Way SN5	12	C3
Roundway Down SN5	18	D1
Rowan Rd. SN2	8	C5
Rowland Hill Clo. SN3	17	G6
Rowton Heath Way SN5	12	C6
Royston Rd. SN3	16	C6
Ruckley Gdns. SN3	10	D6
Rushall Clo. SN2	8	D3
Rushmere Path SN2	8	B3
Blunsdon Rd.		
Rushton Rd. SN3	22	C1
Ruskin Av. SN2	10	B5
Russell Wk. SN3	15	G4
Russley Clo. SN5	12	B1
Ryan Clo. SN5	6	D6
Rycote Clo. SN5	12	C4
Rye Clo. SN5	12	C3

S

Sackville Clo. SN3	16	B3
Saddleback Rd. SN5	12	C3
Sadler Wk. SN3	16	B5
Saffron Clo. SN2	7	F5
Sage Clo. SN2	7	F3
St. Albans Clo. SN2	13	G3
St. Ambrose Clo. SN3	17	F4

St. Andrews Clo. SN4	20	D5
St. Andrews Ct. SN4	20	D5
St. Andrews Grn. SN3	17	G3
St. Helen's Vw. SN1	14	B6
St. Ives Ct. SN3	17	E4
Tyneham Rd.		
St. James Clo. SN2	9	F3
St. John Rd. SN4	20	C6
St. Katherine Grn. SN3	17	G3
St. Margarets Grn. SN3	10	D6
St. Margaret's Retail Pk. SN3	11	F6
St. Margaret's Rd. SN3	21	F1
St. Mary's Gro. SN2	14	D1
St. Paul's Dr. SN3	17	F3
St. Paul's St. SN2	15	E1
St. Phillip's Rd. SN2	9	G5
Salcombe Gro. SN3	16	B5
Salisbury St. SN1	25	F1
Saltram Clo. SN3	17	E4
Salzgitter Dr. SN2	8	D1
Sandacre Rd. SN5	12	B2
Sandgate SN3	16	D1
Sandown Av. SN3	21	G1
Sandpiper Bri. SN3	17	G3
Sandringham Rd. SN3	22	B1
Sanford St. SN1	25	E3
Sarsen Clo. SN1	14	B6
Savernake St. SN1	25	E6
Savill Cres. SN4	20	B5
Saxon Ct. SN3	15	F6
Dammas La.		
Saxton Wk. SN5	12	D2
Marshall Rd.		
Scarborough Rd. SN2	14	B2
School Row SN2	7	G4
Scotby Av. SN3	21	G1
Seagry Ct. SN2	8	D3
Penhill Dr.		
Seaton Clo. SN2	8	B3
Sedgebrook SN3	23	F2
Selby Cres. SN5	12	D6
Semley Wk. SN2	9	E4
Stockton Rd.		
Severn Av. SN2	8	B4
Seymour Rd. SN3	16	B4
Shaftesbury Av. SN3	22	D1
Shakespeare Path SN2	10	B5
Shalbourne Clo. SN2	8	D3
Southwick Av.		
Shanklin Rd. SN2	7	G4
Shaplands SN3	10	C6
Shapwick Clo. SN3	17	E3
Sharp Clo. SN5	12	D3
Shaw Rd. SN5	12	D3

She-Til

Sheen Clo. SN5	12	B6
Lumley Clo.		
Shelfinch SN5	13	F6
Shelley St. SN1	**24**	**C5**
Shenton Clo. SN3	10	D5
Sheppard St. SN1	**24**	**C3**
Sherbourne Pl. SN3	16	D3
Sherford Rd. SN2	7	G4
Sheringham Ct. SN3	23	F1
Grundys		
Sherston Av. SN2	9	E3
Sherwood Clo. SN3	10	D5
Sherwood Rd. SN3	16	D6
Shetland Clo. SN5	12	C3
Shipton Gro. SN3	15	G5
Shire Clo. SN5	12	C3
Shirley Clo. SN3	16	B3
Shrewsbury Rd. SN3	16	B4
Shrewton Wk. SN2	9	E2
Grafton Rd.		
Shrivenham Rd. SN1	**25**	**H3**
Shrivenham Rd. SN3	15	F4
Shropshire Clo. SN5	12	D3
Sidney Clo. SN5	12	B6
Signal Way SN3	21	F1
Silchester Way SN5	13	E4
Silverton Rd. SN3	16	D4
Simnel Clo. SN5	12	B5
Slade Dr. SN3	16	C2
Sleaford Clo. SN5	12	C4
Smitan Brook SN3	17	F4
Snowdrop Clo. SN2	7	F3
Snowshill Clo. SN2	8	B3
Somerdale Clo. SN5	13	E4
Somerford Clo. SN2	9	E4
Somerset Rd. SN2	14	B1
Somerville Rd. SN3	16	B4
Sound Copse SN5	6	D6
South Marston Ind. Est. SN3	11	E1
South St. SN1	15	E6
South Vw. Av. SN3	15	G5
Southampton St. SN1	**25**	**G4**
Southbrook St. SN2	14	D1
Southernwood Dr. SN2	7	E4
Southwick Av. SN2	8	D3
Sparcells Dr. SN5	6	D6
Speedwell Clo. SN2	7	G3
Cloudberry Rd.		
Spencer Clo. SN5	12	B3
Spenser Clo. SN3	16	C3
Spheresholt SN5	13	F6
Spindle Tree Ct. SN2	8	D6
Spring Gdns. SN1	**25**	**F3**
Springfield Rd. SN1	21	E1
Springhill Clo. SN5	13	E5
Spruce Ct. SN2	8	D6
Spur Way SN2	9	G5
Square, The SN1	15	F6

Squires Copse SN5	12	C1
Squires Gate SN2	8	B2
Stafford St. SN1	**24**	**D6**
Stamford Clo. SN5	12	D5
Stanbridge Pk. SN5	12	C3
Berkshire Dr.		
Stancombe Pk. SN5	12	C2
Standings Clo. SN5	12	C2
Standon Way SN2	8	D1
Stanier St. SN1	**24**	**D5**
Stanley St. SN1	**25**	**F6**
Stanmore St. SN1	**24**	**B6**
Stansfield Clo. SN5	13	E6
Stanway Clo. SN3	16	C6
Stapleford Clo. SN2	8	D2
Stapleford Way SN2	8	D2
Ramsbury Av.		
Staring Clo. SN5	12	B2
Station Rd. SN1	**24**	**D2**
Staverton Way SN2	9	E2
Westwood Rd.		
Stedham Wk. SN3	16	D6
Whitbourne Av.		
Stennes Clo. SN5	7	E6
Stephens Rd. SN3	16	C2
Stephenson Rd. SN2	9	E1
Stirling Clo. SN4	20	C5
Stirling Rd. SN3	11	E2
Stockbridge Copse SN5	6	D6
Stockton Rd. SN2	9	E4
Stokesay Dr. SN5	13	E6
Stone La. SN5	6	A6
Stonecrop Way SN2	7	G3
Stonefield Clo. SN5	13	E4
Stonehill Grn. SN5	13	F4
Stonehurst Rd. SN3	16	C2
Stonybeck Clo. SN5	13	F4
Stour Rd. SN2	8	D4
Stour Wk. SN2	8	D4
Severn Av.		
Stratford Clo. SN5	13	F5
Stratton Orchard SN3	10	C6
Stratton Rd. SN1	16	B2
Stratton Rd. SN3	16	B2
Stratton St. Margaret Bypass SN2	9	F2
Street, The SN2	7	G5
Street, The SN5	12	A2
Stuart Clo. SN3	16	B4
Stubsmead SN3	17	E5
Studland Clo. SN3	22	D1
Sudeley Way SN5	12	C5
Suffolk St. SN2	15	E2
Summerhouse Rd. SN4	20	C5
Summers St. SN2	14	B3
Sunningdale Rd. SN2	9	E4
Sunnyside Av. SN1	14	C6
Surrey Rd. SN2	14	C1

Sussex Sq. SN3	16	B4
Somerville Rd.		
Sutton Rd. SN3	17	E6
Swallowdale SN3	17	F3
Swallowfield Av. SN3	16	B5
Swanage Wk. SN2	7	G5
Branksome Rd.		
Swanbrook SN3	17	F2
Swindon Rd. SN1	**25**	**E6**
Swindon Rd. SN3	16	C1
Swindon Rd. SN4	20	D5
Swinley Dr. SN5	6	C6
Sycamore Gro. SN2	9	E6
Symonds SN5	18	D1
Syon Clo. SN2	8	B2
Sywell Rd. SN3	17	E2

T

Tallis Wk. SN5	12	C5
Ascham Rd.		
Tamar Clo. SN2	8	C4
Tamworth Dr. SN5	12	C3
Tansley Moor SN3	23	G1
Taplow Wk. SN3	16	C6
Priory Rd.		
Tarragon Clo. SN2	7	E4
Tattershall SN5	19	E1
Taunton St. SN1	**24**	**B4**
Tavistock Rd. SN3	16	D4
Tawny Owl Clo. SN3	17	E2
Taylor Cres. SN3	10	C4
Tealsbrook SN3	17	F3
Techno Trd. Est. SN2	16	B1
Tedder Clo. SN3	8	D6
Tees Clo. SN2	8	C4
Teeswater Clo. SN5	12	C4
Telford Way SN5	13	F6
Temple St. SN1	**25**	**E5**
Tenby Clo. SN3	22	B1
Tennyson St. SN1	**24**	**C5**
Tenzing Gdns. SN2	9	E5
Terncliff SN3	17	F3
Tewkesbury Way SN5	12	B3
Thackeray Clo. SN3	17	F6
Thames Av. SN2	7	G3
Theatre Sq. SN1	**25**	**E4**
Theobald St. SN1	**24**	**C4**
Thirlmere SN3	23	G1
Thomas St. SN2	14	B3
Thornbridge Av. SN3	16	C6
Thorne Rd. SN3	17	E6
Thornford Dr. SN5	13	E5
Thornhill Ind. Est. SN3	11	G5
Thornhill Rd. SN3	11	F4
Thrushel Clo. SN2	7	G4
Thurlestone Rd. SN3	15	G5
Thurney Dr. SN5	12	B6
Thyme Clo. SN2	7	E5
Tilley's La. SN3	10	C6
Tilshead Wk. SN2	8	D3

This index is also available on floppy disk with

THE BARTHOLOMEW INDEXMASTER

The index to street or place names on a map or atlas is a vital part of the overall map information. It enables the user to locate the grid square in which the place they are looking for is situated.

All too often however the position of the index can create problems. It is usually printed on the reverse side of the map so that when the product is laid out flat on a table or mounted on the wall the index is no longer visible.

In street atlases, the index often has to be printed in very small text to fit within the space allowed, so it can be difficult to read. Then of course it is always possible to misread an entry particularly when there are twenty 'Station Roads' or 'High Streets'!....there is no doubt reading an index can be a painstaking and often frustrating routine.

IndexMaster is a piece of software available from Bartholomew which enables streets on the map to be located quickly using the home or office personal computer.

The software can be 'bundled' on disk with the index for any street map or atlas from the Nicholson and Bartholomew range. When it is loaded onto a PC, the user can simply type in the street or place name required and it will be highlighted on the screen with its grid reference in seconds.....no more searching, squinting and frustration.

Besides being able to find rapidly any streets in the index, with IndexMaster, it is possible to add additional locations. For instance, a taxi company might like to add their own choice of popular destinations in a variety of colours, for example pubs in green, hospitals in red and police stations in blue. There are many ways of customising the index to individual specifications.

IndexMaster, which is simple to install and operate, runs under Microsoft Windows 3.0 and higher, on all IBM and 100% compatible PCs.

For further details contact
Department EP, Bartholomew, Cheltenham:

Telephone - (01242) 512748
Fax   - (01242) 222725